G000068012

PHOTOGRAPHIC CREDITS

FRONT COVER PHOTOGRAPH © DEREK RIDGERS, © LONDON FEATURES INTERNATIONAL
© ALL ACTION
© LONDON FEATURES INTERNATIONAL LTD
© REX FEATURES

UFO Music Ltd 18 Hanway Street London W1P 9DD England
Telephone: 0171 636 1281   Fax: 0171 636 0738

First published in Great Britain 1997
UFO Music Ltd 18 Hanway Street
London W1P 9DD

The author and publishers have made every effort to contact all copyright holders. Any who for any reason have not been contacted are invited to write to the publishers so that a full acknowledgment may be made in subsequent editions of this work.

ISBN 1-873884-85-0

Designed by UFO Music Ltd

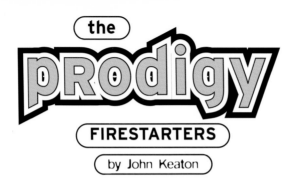

FIRESTARTERS

by John Keaton

Well, you've got Liverpool: the Beatles, obviously, Merseybeat, Echo & The Bunnymen, The La's, a million and one Frankie Says! T-shirts stuck in a million and one bottom drawers, scallies with guitars, you know the form. Then there's Manchester, and who doesn't know about Manchester? Here they come, from the Buzzcocks through Joy Division, down to The Smiths, round to the Mondays and the Stone Roses, until you get to Oasis. London? Easy; the Who, the Stones, the Clash, the Pistols. Each one convinced of the greatness of its history, its contribution to what's kept the nation on its toes over the last few decades. Bristol, Glasgow, Sheffield. They've all had a go. Braintree never gets much of a mention.

Still hamstrung by its reputation, Essex. Still so often the punchline. Maybe now's the time for Essex to assert itself and take (over)due credit. Throughout the seventies, while the rest of the country argued over the relative merits of gobshite punk rockers and frankly embarrassing prog-hippies, Essex was founding a tradition of dance. The world at large barely gave the burgeoning soul scene a second glance, and much the same fate befell the tightknit cluster of jazz-funk and electro devotees; their day would be a long time coming. Nobody seemed remotely interested in this strange little corner of England, with its DJs and import 12"s. Not yet. But Essex knew.

So, it should have come as no great surprise, as the eighties dragged to a close, to find that Essex was once again leading the way in dance music; the difference was, this time people were listening. On a wave of media attention the underground found itself starting to break big, and, on this occasion, the underground was going by the name of Acid House. Taking its cue from the earliest Detroit techno of Derrick May, it was minimalist, purpose built to dance to, its musical focus the original repetitive beat.

The music, however, was only part of the story; Britain, and in particular the Essex kids fortuitously close to the Dutch sea ports, had discovered ecstasy. The music and the pills worked in tandem to create an entire culture, one revolving around elusive all-nighters, warehouses and service stations, pirate radio and waiting for the phone to ring and let you know what was going on and, more importantly, where. And let's not forget the smileys, beaming up from, it seemed, every flyer there ever was.

The M25 was the key. Around it, outside one of London's satellite towns, you'd find the party, or at least enough people shivering expectantly by the roadside to tell you it was in the offing. Once again, on the edge of the orbital, there was Essex: you could call it a case of right place, right time.

start the dance

start the dance
start the dance
dance

1989 WITNESSED WHAT WAS SOMETIMES CALLED THE "SECOND SUMMER OF LOVE" as the E kicked in against a soundtrack of squelchy, acidic house. The growing popularity of both the music and the culture contrasted with the feverish denunciations of them by local authorities, fretting about noise levels, the tabloid press, whipping up hysteria over this new "dance drug", and the music industry - where were the stars? But, in the clubs, it was what the crowd wanted to hear, wanted to spend the night with.

One such club was the Barn, just outside Braintree, whose resident DJ was a certain Mr C. At the earliest raves held there, much of the attention was focused on a trio of dancers, all displaying their moves and all fairly obviously well into the spirit of things. The first, Sharky, a girl who'd been around the parties since they'd first started taking place; the second was Leeroy Thornhill, tall and some might say gangling, a well known face around the raves, his dancing owing more to his teenage fixation with James Brown than the running on the spot while gurning style of his peers; the third, Keith Flint, substantially shorter than Leeroy, a former Essex casual and self-confessed hooligan with what could be called a chequered past, threatened with expulsion from school and without a qualification to his name. Years later he would tell an interviewer that:

> **"I admit my school results were terrible. If it weren't for the Prodigy, God knows what I'd be doing."**

Keith had been away, travelling round Europe and Africa, and had become an unapologetic hippy; when he got back to Britain, he found the party had already started.

This motley crew had become a firm fixture within the scene by the time Keith found himself at an all-nighter, outdoors, doing his thing to a DJ whose decks were set up in a transit van. Always the epitome of loved up sociability, Keith immediately befriended the man dropping the tunes, a shy figure who had only recently allowed the new sound to supplant his first love, of hip hop. The DJ was Liam Howlett. Liam's musical background took in eight years of childhood piano lessons, an early fondness for ska and Two Tone, and an adolescence spent increasingly wrapped up in, first, electro and breakdancing, before following the logical progression towards hip hop; Liam did like his hip hop.

The trouble was, being a white boy from Braintree into hip hop brought Liam a lot of grief. Granted, he could let his shyness pass itself off as inscrutability and he knew his tunes inside out, but he still never came to feel accepted within the fraternity: he just ended up on the wrong end of a lot of attitude. His decks had been paid for by stints working as a labourer, and he'd managed to get himself hooked up with a Chelmsford hip hop outfit, Cut to Kill, acting as their second DJ. Even that had just brought him grief, though.

A guy he'd been working for had helped buy studio time, and Cut to Kill duly recorded twelve tracks, pressing up fifty copies on vinyl and sending them out, as is the tradition, to those they hoped would become interested parties: labels, agents, promoters. Equally traditionally, they had no joy whatsoever, and it was only several months later that Tam Tam, at that point one of the UK's leading hip hop labels (not that they had much competition), got in touch, Cut to Kill having followed up their demo LP with another offering, written by Liam. The only snag being that the deal they were offered didn't actually include him. Maybe it was time for pastures new.

Liam had already started to overcome his initial dislike of house, finding that the music, the drugs and the parties were starting to work their magic on his original indifference. His own material was becoming more and more influenced by the sub-bass and multi-rhythmic repetitions he was hearing, and it was these tunes he recorded onto the flipside of a mix tape of his set. The mix tape in question had been requested by the funny little guy Liam had encountered at the party, Keith Flint; at some point the following morning, having just got back from Raindance, then one of the country's most popular raves, Keith and Leeroy decided to give the tape a go. Liam's tunes came forth from the stereo; our boys were blown clean away. They were so into the sounds, they hardly noticed the name written on the side of the tape case, The Prodigy, after Liam's beloved

Moog Prodigy keyboard. It was a job well done; Keith and Leeroy were thoroughly smitten.

By the time they next ran into Liam, predictably enough at the Barn, they'd decided on his behalf that he should start doing live work, with the two of them and Sharky dancing for him. Scrutinising the odd couple in front of him, Liam agreed that, no, it wasn't such a bad idea; he'd already concluded that playing live should be the next step in his post-Cut to Kill career, and was well aware that him standing there, tinkering at his keyboard, was hardly going to make for the most gripping show there ever was. Something was still missing, however. Dancers were a start, but if it was going to work, he'd need an MC. Not that he knew anyone even remotely suitable.

Once again, the busy hand of fate was able to help out. Persuading Ziggy, a friend with enough all-important connections, that he should help manage the newly formed Prodigy was a definite stroke of luck. Not only was he able to get them their first PA, at a club called The Labyrinth in deepest, darkest Dalston, he also made a couple of calls to track down a guy he knew who might just fit the bill perfectly for the situation vacant as Master of Ceremonies. Keith Palmer, otherwise known as Keeti, or, when he'd started chatting over reggae sound systems in his native Peterborough, Maxim Reality; maybe he'd be interested. Maxim, like Liam, had a grounding in hip hop, but he was really more of a reggae man, having moved down to London with the express intention of getting himself a rep as an MC, in the mould of Papa San, Supercat and the like. While unsure about what exactly he could do over this bunch of Essex ravers his mate Ziggy had told him about, Liam seemed sound enough from the brief conversation they'd had to

confirm his involvement, and, at the very least, doing the Labyrinth should be, well, interesting.

Even then, Liam knew he actually wanted to play live, as opposed to just letting the tapes run while he mimed at his keyboard. Fuck that. It didn't really make that much difference to Keith, Leeroy and Sharky; they spent the week before the PA rehearsing and perfecting their moves, becoming thoroughly acquainted with the nuances of the tunes so that they'd be a visual accompaniment to the music, rather than just a distraction from Liam. In addition to working on their dancing, the three also ran up some costumes; green and white, with a large contrasting circle in the centre of the chest, they would come across, amid the strobes and lights and beats and bleeps, like a trio of rave court jesters, a blur of motion done up in latter-day harlequin outfits, although Liam would later observe that they made them "look like the Stylistics." It was all starting to fall into place, even if none of them had actually met Maxim yet, their only contact being Liam's call to tell him where they were playing, and the tape which had come through his letter box a couple of days later.

When they did finally meet, it was about four hours to showtime at the Labyrinth. Everyone was getting nervy; only Maxim was acquainted with the routine and rigmarole of playing live, and he was the one who had only just found out the order of the eight song set, throughout which he would be obliged to improvise, having received little in the way of "creative direction". Nobody's mood was greatly lifted by the news, jovially imparted to them by the club's owner, that the Labyrinth had only ever put on one PA before, and that had ended in a hail of beer bottles. Yep, it was certainly going to be interesting; so interesting, in fact, that Keith and Leeroy thought they might just help the proceedings along by going halves on an E shortly before going on. They soon learnt that while a pill may have inspired them into ever more complex moves and a greater feeling of purposeful unity at the Barn, dancing onstage, with 250 people looking directly at you, that was a completely different matter.

The infant Prodigy had managed to pull in a fair smattering of familiar faces from the Essex parties, as well as a number of actual paying punters. Once they got over the vague paranoia they felt at first, Leeroy and Keith, with Sharky alongside them, managed to dance up a storm. Liam was positioned at the back, playing and triggering samples. Maxim stood beside him, chatting where he thought it was appropriate, although still somewhat confused over whether he was doing what he was supposed to. All things considered, it was a success; they got asked back to play a Saturday, a fortnight later, they'd gone down well, and none of them had been on the receiving end of any beer bottles. They were away, and before they next turned up in Dalston, Maxim had had some guidance over his role: he would remain as the Prodigy's MC, but would try to strip down his vocal style to complement the music, cutting back on the elaborations and freestyling he'd learnt on the reggae and hip hop scene while maintaining a constant human presence within Liam's tunes.

The show at the Labyrinth established a precedent for the rest of the Prodigy's trajectory upwards and onwards. They would play live, no tapes, and they would play more or less anywhere that would have them, irrespective of the size or makeup of their audience. Although Sharky would soon quit the band, in the most amicable of fashions, wanting to go to raves rather than play at them, that thing called chemistry was already coming into effect. There was Keith and Leeroy at the front of the stage, always dancing, always moving, providing a mirror to the audience (although following the first show, they thought it best all round to give the E a skip from then on), Maxim adding an element of menace and swagger, the man with the mic, and there was Liam. And Liam, even if he would only admit it reluctantly, saw that he might just have stumbled onto something which would give his music and his talent a shot at getting heard.

Both in terms of their live act and Liam's material, with its union of techno - already taking over from the more mannered, minimalist sound of house - and hip hop influenced breakbeats, the Prodigy were going about things differently to their contemporaries. Without much in the way of a masterplan, they ran things off the cuff: if they were asked to play, they'd play, and if the audience was non-committal before, on most occasions they were converts afterwards. It stood them in good stead, the Labyrinth, it set the tone. Seven years on, one of Britain's biggest bands, on the verge of cracking what so many guitar hopefuls have tried and failed to do, getting America to sit up and listen, commercially huge and critically respected, you can still see that, essentially, it's much the same arrangement. Liam's tunes, Maxim, Keith and Leeroy the nutters providing him with the perfect foil.
Start the dance.

in the fastlane
in the fastlane
in the fastlane
in the fastlane
in the fastlane

chapter two

THE AVOWED POLICY OF PLAYING ANYWHERE AND EVERY WHERE WAS BEGINNING TO PAY OFF, but success breeds success; shortly after the first PA at the Labyrinth, Liam manged to pull off something of a coup in ensuring the Prodigy's continued ascent. He got himself a deal.

From the original tape handed to Keith, which the rest of the band were still using as their blueprint for their PAs, Liam had narrowed the selection down to four tunes, and duly despatched a copy to Tam Tam. We can only wonder whether the label's then A&R department can still be found gnashing their teeth and tearfully kicking themselves, as, despite Cut to Kill having been signed on the back of Liam's material, the tape wasn't deemed good enough for a deal to be struck.

Strike one. Strike two involved a relatively new underground dance label, XL. Liam overcame his shyness long enough to call up one of the label heads, Nick Halkes, blag himself a meeting at the company's South London offices, and with it the chance to play his stuff. The meeting itself went reasonably well, Halkes listening attentively to the four tracks Liam had chosen to represent him, as well as sizing up the quietly-spoken songwriter himself, giving him the chance to explain what he was all about. Liam was pleased to have been given the opportunity to do some sizing up himself, a chance to learn what record companies really wanted, but didn't expect much more. This was only the second label he'd contacted, and he wasn't too surprised when Halkes' immediate response, while friendly enough, fell firmly into the category of "right then, we'll be in touch".

A week later, to Liam's surprise, XL did get in touch, offering the Prodigy a singles deal, to be signed, sealed and delivered as quickly as possible. The first release was to be a 12" of the four tunes Halkes had heard during his meeting with Liam, among them an early mix of Everybody In The Place. The main cut, however, was to be What Evil Lurks, a brooding slab of techno taking its title from a sample of 40s radio series The Shadow, and piling on the breakbeats which gave the whole track a verve and originality which much dance music was already sacrificing in the name of floor filler. What Nick Halkes and XL had seen in Liam was what the rest of us would find out soon enough: that he was capable of performing that trickiest of tightrope walks, balancing a genuine underground sensibility and aural viciousness with an ear for what people might actually choose to listen to.

While the rest of the band were mightily impressed by the speed with which Liam had secured an outlet for his tunes, they could be forgiven for being somewhat nonplussed. Keith in particular was in it for the dancing, the buzz of being up on stage, rocking the crowd; he hadn't expected record deals. His personal ambitions as part of the Prodigy, in fact, didn't extend much beyond playing Raindance, at that point regarded as probably the country's biggest and best outdoor rave. His other plans included a return to travel those parts of the world he'd missed out on the first time; by the time Liam told him about XL and the imminent release of What Evil Lurks, he'd already booked his flight to Thailand.

Fortunately for all concerned, Keith subsequently fell victim to a remarkable run of bad luck, involving the theft of all his travel money and, just to round things off nicely, getting himself nicked in Soho Square for smoking what the arresting officer later described to the magistrate's court as a "large roll-up cigarette", and not the kind of large roll-up cigarette you generally see being partaken of on the streets of central London. Cancelling his flight, it looked as though the Prodigy was going to be able to hang onto its dancers after all.

What Evil Lurks proved that the Prodigy could shift records, selling, with minimal promotion, 7000 copies over the next few weeks. It's now something of a collector's item, changing hands (when it can be found) for well over £100. The release of the record worked in tandem with the band's constant gigging to keep on raising their profile within the underground. A DJ would play at least one of the four tracks on the EP at a club or party, the next time the promoter was booking a PA he or she would remember the way the menacing tune had moved the crowd so efficiently and get on the phone to Liam or Ziggy, the Prodigy would play, DJs and ravers alike would find themselves blown away by the increasingly frenetic and (dare we say it) professional show, get hold of a copy of the record, the DJ would try it in his set the next time he played, and so on and so forth. Things were moving fast.

the jilted generation
the jilted generation
the jilted generation
the jilted generation
generation

chapter three

**THE RELEASE OF THE WHAT EVIL LURKS 12"
CONSUMMATED THE RELATIONSHIP BETWEEN THE
PRODIGY AND XL.** The band respected the label's
attitude, never interfering with Liam's writing or
attempting to cajole them into making fools of
themselves in the name of promotion, while the label
were never less than impressed with the quality of
Liam's tunes, their ceaseless workrate when it came
to gigs and the fact that their records increasingly
began to sell by the proverbial bucketload. It's
proved to be a happy marriage, with Richard
Russell, the Managing Director of XL, expressing his
reasoning for the Prodigy's success thus:

*"They have two great frontmen in Keith and
Maxim...they're also both innovative and populist... I
feel Liam, as a producer and a musician is just a
genius. He's doing something that's completely
sonically different and out there."*

The feeling's mutual; after being wooed by Island, following
the big sales and critical plaudits collected by Music for the

Jilted Generation, Liam decided to stick with XL, explaining that:

"I have complete freedom to do what I want at XL which I might not have somewhere else, so why change things?"

In fact, the only real black spot besmirching the Prodigy's dealings with record companies came in the States. During a jaunt across the Atlantic in the spring of '92 they were spotted by a scout from LA's Elektra, a label which prided itself on its history of signing and developing fresh and radical sounding talent. The Prodigy were rapidly snapped up.

Things didn't really work out. The first LP, Experience, had failed to take off and, in marked contrast to their increasingly unassailable position in the UK and Europe, the Prodigy found themselves stuck in a vicious circle which will be horribly familiar to countless Brit bands: they didn't sell, their relationship with the label deteriorated, they weren't promoted, they didn't sell. Unlike XL, Elektra were persistent in their attempts to steer Liam's music this way or that, chronically unsure over whether there was any market in the sprawl of the Mid-West for hard dance from the South East of England. Shortly after Jilted Generation began to take over the airwaves and homes of Britain, Elektra dropped the Prodigy.

Not for the first time, you're struck by images of apologetic label executives trying desperately to account for their complete lack of foresight. When the video for

Firestarter grabbed the holy grail of the US music business, heavy rotation on MTV, and the import only 12" began to fly out of the shops, the Prodigy, having been without an American deal for almost two years, suddenly found themselves the subject of an intense bidding war between at least twenty different labels - although, presumably, this didn't include Elektra.

In the autumn of '96, they signed with Madonna's label, Maverick, for what was rumoured to be worth over £2 million to the band over the next five years. Asked why they had gone for Maverick, the band's reasoning was simple; a spokesman for them justified their love by saying that:

> *"Madonna just knew more about the techno scene than anyone else."*

charly charly says
charly says says

"We're out there to rock a crowd and that's all we care about" - Liam

HOWEVER AWESOME THE RECORDS, however, as anyone who's seen the adrenalised, all singing, all dancing, whirling dervish that is the Prodigy live will tell you, for them it's as much about what happens on stage as in a darkened studio. It was playing live, despite never rehearsing (they did try it the once, but it went so badly that it remained just the once), that cemented their following, gave them the edge over what competition they had. It's worth remembering that while most rock bands spend their entire careers playing to single figure audiences, the ones hailed as stars are those who finally reach the point of performing in front of 10,000 people; when Keith got his wish and the Prodigy played at Raindance, that's the number of people who watched them. It was their eleventh gig.

The video for Charly, the surreal hardcore anthem which took them overground (at least to the extent of selling 200,000 copies and reaching number 3 in the charts) was as good a indicator as any of what is often quaintly referred to as "stage presence". There they were, on a stage, somewhere, Keith and Leeroy already well versed in the art of bigging up an audience, still in their matching green and white costumes as they just kept on dancing, Liam at his keyboard, the maestro. Maxim had yet to assert himself, but he would, he most certainly would.

25

The constant round of gigs and PAs left them polished, albeit polished in the most maniacal way imaginable. There wasn't a show or an audience which could intimidate them; why fret about Glastonbury when you promoted your first few singles by playing to tens of thousands on a regular basis? In Leeroy, Maxim and Keith, oh yes, especially Keith, Liam had chanced upon three true showmen. Their background in rave had also left them with an appreciation that playing live should give an audience more than just the opportunity to gawp at the band; by the time Experience had come out, the Prodigy were already playing through their own 50 K sound system, backed up with an array of 3D heliographic lasers, computer animation and interactive lighting.

The show just got more and more intense, coming to resemble a cyberpunk slapstick horror flick of beats and madness. Liam became the hub, standing at the back of the stage, surrounded by his gadgetry and, by the time of the Jilted Generation tour, a drum kit and a cage to boot. Keith would bait the audience, every inch the techno imp, stagediving at will and, eventually, taking the stage in a man-sized hamster ball (and yes, the Prodigy are fans of Spinal Tap). Maxim had developed a mean presence of his own, sparring with Keith and, when the mood took him, flashing his cat's eyes contact lenses down at the crowd; when asked where the idea came from, he replied:

"I don't know, I just like intimidating people."

And in the midst of it all, Leeroy, still loping along to his own beat.

For the Jilted shows the band also recruited a guitarist, Gizz Butt, whose past included plying his trade in punk rock warhorses such as The Destructors and English Dogs. The culture clash was just another facet of the inspired lunacy of their live act, and also acted as a pointer towards the incredibly eclectic, crossover nature of their tastes and, increasingly, their audience. You had a grim, almost industrial set, strobes and lasers, ravers on stage and a guy in a studded leather jacket with a guitar. Hardly any wonder that the NME, by now enthusiastic in the extreme, said of the Prodigy live that they were:

"Unique - the only band who can create the unified, triumphant atmosphere of an Ibiza rave at the same time as delivering all the elements of a great rock gig."

By the time they came to do their UK shoes of 1996, they felt like a change of scene. Rather than losing any edge, however, ditching their quasi-industrial set just added to the show's demented majesty. This time, they'd be playing on a stage furnished with a fish tank, a bank of seventies TV sets, each one methodically tuned to static, a pink fun fur telephone, framed pictures including the band's ant logo and the granny from the Firestarter sleeve, mocked up windows which would act as projectors, three ornamental fish on the back wall and several enormous lampshades, the whole thing set off to perfection by a gruesome retro carpet in glorious shades of orange, purple and brown. As live performance goes, it sure beats watching some anonymous blokes perfecting their pouts in the back room of a Camden pub.

While it was no surprise to see them ending the year as winners of Select's award for Best Live Act, and runners up (to the ubiquitous Oasis) in the equivalent NME poll, playing live for the Prodigy always was far more than simply a device to promote their records, and, therefore, rare indeed would be the audience member who could ever say, hand on heart, that they were just going through the motions. Liam still loved having the simple opportunity to put his tunes across, and the band as a whole still got their kicks in much the same way as they had when dancing at the Barn in Essex. As Keith has said:

"That's why we do it, because it's such a fucking buzz...before we went on stage at Brixton, you couldn't have injected me with any drug that would've made me feel better than that. Any more than that and I would've felt ill - my head wouldn't have been able to handle it! It was like tripping to the max."

The only people with a history of not enjoying their slice of live Prodigy are security men. Not known for their sense of humour, Keith and Maxim have both found themselves, on more than one occasion, being refused entry back onto the stage by over-zealous security, having dived into the crowd. There have also been anxious promoters and insurers, terrified by the thought of what could happen to Keith as he crowd surfs. Throughout their career, in fact, the only grief Keith has suffered while engaging with the audience came at the

hands of our old friends the security men:
at one notable show in Newcastle, for
instance, Liam, Leeroy and Maxim found it
virtually impossible to keep straight faces
as they observed their bandmate
attempting to haul himself back up on
stage, being mistaken for just another
punter, and, in the confusion, having his
trousers pulled down by the security guard,
eager to remove him. Rock and roll.

Such embarrassment notwithstanding, the Prodigy still relish playing live. That's
when the pent-up aggression and energy inherent within the high voltage tunes
gets its release. It's a rep they've earned, and one they're justifiably proud of. As far
as Liam's concerned:

*"The live act is what we're all about. We've dedicated
the last five years of our lives to it, so we don't just
want a polite round of applause at the end of a show. We
want to stir people up so much that they have to be
carried out, exhausted, on a stretcher."*

Got that?

31

everybody in the place
everybody in the place
everybody in the place
everybody in the place
everybody in the place

THE PRODIGY FOLLOWED UP ON CHARLY WITH EVERYBODY IN THE PLACE, another furious slab of breakbeat techno, a raver's anthem, its stuttering rhythms at once harder and more insistently uplifting than those of its predecessors. The video featured the boys strutting their stuff on the streets of New York, where they had just done their first American PA at the infamous Limelight club, fitting right in, or at least trying to, alongside the various drag queens and S&M enthusiasts who made up the club's staple crowd.

Despite mainstream radio's continued apathy towards them - it wasn't anything personal, no radio station other than the pirates was ever less than entirely dismissive of rave and techno - and their refusal to appear on Top of the Pops (already demonstrating their deterninedly anti-commercial stance, one they've always maintained), Everybody In The Place managed to outdo even Charly in terms of commercial success, reaching number 2 in the charts in the run up to Christmas '91. Sadly enough, it was only kept off the top by the re-release of Queen's Bohemian Rhapsody: may the British record buying public hang their heads in shame.

The constant round of gigs remained the Prodigy's central method throughout much of the following year, up and down the country and frequently over to Europe, their regular schedule involving at least three shows a week. It was several months before their next release, a cover of the sixties novelty hit Fire, originally performed by the Crazy World of Arthur Brown. An ironic dig at the expense of those who had written them off as a novelty band themselves, or just something which lent itself to a good honest techno going-over? Whatever, its release was significant for a number of reasons.

For a start, it was their first release since XL had confirmed their intention to put out a Prodigy album. When they had first hooked up with the label, dance music's primary currency was, as it still is, the 12" single; it was music designed exclusively for five or so minutes of mayhem at a rave, not the kind of repeated, sitting at home listening that was associated with albums. And did any of this wave of techno bands have enough quality material to stretch beyond the club or the party? By this stage, the Prodigy's peers were beginning to drop away: Shades of Rhythm, N Joi, Altern 8, all were finding it tricky to keep up their momentum.

XL, however, felt that in the Prodigy, and in particular in Liam Howlett, they had the requisite quality. A wise decision. The debut LP was already pretty much done and dusted by the time Fire came out to trail its release. Another reason for the importance of its release came in the form of its flipside, Horns of Jericho; while Fire was nagging enough, displaying the kind of uncompromising eerieness which would become a trademark of much of the Prodigy's work, it was Jericho which was to be the LP's opening gambit, the toughest thing the band had done by a long way. Screaming and screeching, a harsh collision of hard beats and bone-shaking bass, it gained Liam a large measure of respect from London's underground. Hardcore techno was beginning its slow but sure evolution into jungle, an altogether more serious creature, and the new scene's forerunners nodded in approval at the badness that was Horns of Jericho: DJs such as Fabio and Ray Keith, now widely esteemed in drum & bass circles, were among the first to pick up on the tune, while it was remixed by proto-junglists Genaside II.

This juggling act of keeping it real while still selling would characterise The Prodigy's development. Their headstrong belief that they could rock any crowd you'd care to mention was tested and proven by their appearance, around the release of Fire, at Sheffield Sound City, an otherwise wholly indie festival, playing with (and duly blowing off stage) the likes of Suede and Ned's Atomic Dustbin. No-one else would have even attempted such a move, but the Prodigy pulled it off in style; the NME was moved to describe them as:

"A riot...a compulsive, multi-faceted entertainment extravaganza...the future is now."

Everything was in place for the release of the album, and, when it came, Experience didn't disappoint. Already a considerable distance from any accusations of novelty status, the depth and variety of the material was apparent. You had Jericho, you had the feelgood techno of Your Love, the crazed skank of Out of Space, a remix of Charly that more or less took the original to pieces and started over (binning the feline Charly himself), the hallucinatory, almost ambient Weather Experience, a sure sign of Liam's versatility and imagination. It was everything XL and the band's followers could have hoped for, the nearest thing to a definitive statement of what the raves had created as the soon-to-be jilted generation would get, an early nineties Quadrophenia or Never Mind The Bollocks. Oh, it also managed to sell over 200,000 copies in Britain alone, and half that again worldwide.

But, despite the success of Experience, life was about to get a touch more problematic for the band; although they could be forgiven for thinking they were leading charmed lives, they were about to discover that things were seldom that straightforward. For the first time they found themselves playing to half-full venues; the 23 date tour to support the release of the album represented a transition into playing sizeable concert halls such as Glasgow's Barrowlands and the Aston Villa Leisure Centre in Birmingham. The tour was notable more for its disasters than its successes: in Coventry, they managed to cause a power failure throughout most of the city

centre, while in Folkestone, a ticket-less
punter rather rudely interrupted the show by falling
through the venue's glass roof having attempted to watch the gig
from above. Caught somewhere between two stools, a step away from the
outdoor raves they'd grown up in, but not quite yet accepted by the more
traditional gig-going audience of students and rock fans, these shows were more or
less the first they had played to any significant amount of empty space.

Undeterred, they set off on another, even more ill-fated five date jaunt, this time to Australia. The
problem was, the band who'd play with anyone and anywhere were obliged to face up to the fact
that others weren't so sure of themselves. They were sharing a bill with two British DJs, Sasha and
Paul Oakenfold, the latter convinced of his own star quality, the former not far behind. A long way from
home, and a long way from the unity of the rave, the shows were punctuated by squabbles and
bickering, Sasha and Oakenfold's noses being put out of joint by the presence of these Essex louts,
although, just maybe, it could also have had something to do with the ferocity of the Prodigy's set
in comparison with the tepid house by numbers served up by the two celebrity DJs.

It would get worse, though. It did, as soon as they got to America. The band were tied to
a formidable schedule of playing 28 shows in 30 days, which, bearing in mind the
amount of travel involved, meant they would never be out of each other's
sight, either playing, travelling or sleeping. The Prodigy may not have
been your typical English hopefuls, but they found their first
trek across the often barren U.S. every bit as
arduous and aggravating as

everybody in the place

their many predecessors. While New York and a handful of college towns were beginning to clue themselves into techno, the rest of the States was less receptive; the hick towns of the Mid-West demonstrated their notorious ignorance of anything but lighters-in-the-air guitar boogie, and the country as a whole, with its strict pigeonholes and categorisation, just couldn't come to terms with these British white boys playing frantic, electronic dance music.

About the only laughs they could muster came from winding up their tourmate Moby, a non-smoking, anti-drugs teetotal vegan. The two acts weren't what you'd call soulmates, and their tour bus came to resemble a month long school trip, the Prodigy the naughty boys taking up the back seats. Playing to crowds where the best they could hope for was mild curiosity, being physically threatened in LA when they complained about their treatment, losing money, they only persevered through sheer bloody-mindedness, and the desire not to disappoint those people who did want to see them, few as they were; by the end of the tour, they were not a happy bunch. Even Leeroy made no secret of being seriously pissed off with the whole enterprise, and when the normally super-laid back Leeroy was driven to complaining, the rest of the band knew things must be getting bad.

The only relief came with the flight back to London. Shortly after their return, Wind It Up was pulled off the LP, remixed and released as a single (complete with a video featuring footage of Keith on LA's Venice Beach, where, as if to sum up the entire sorry nature of the American tour, he almost managed to get himself killed by a 20 foot tidal wave). Despite the by-now customary commercial success of the single, Liam was anxious that the track, by now over a year old, wasn't a true reflection of his musical direction, the tunes he was now writing less easy to classify as simply 'rave', displaying the expansiveness and scope which Experience had hinted at. Times were changing.

earthbound

"I want to surprise people every time a Prodigy record comes out" - Liam

In the summer of '93, a white label tune bearing little information on its sleeve other than an address, and the name 'Earthbound', began doing the rounds. It was swiftly picked up on by a hugely impressed dance scene, DJs regularly dropping it into their sets, and specialist shops being scoured for available copies. The track was a tangle of rhythms, pulsing house meeting almost shamanistic percussion; over the beats was a sample of Arabic muezzin wailing and sudden, virtually orchestral, stabs of keyboards. While such uncredited white labels were a permanent fixture in a world where the new style was always the most sought after of prizes, Earthbound attracted a startling amount of praise and attention, as well as a degree of curiosity over who exactly had produced the tune.

The answer came when it emerged that Earthbound was none other than one Liam Howlett. Eager to put out something which indicated the fresh direction the Prodigy were taking, and even keener not to have it weighed down by the snobbery the band had received in the wake of their commercial success, it worked a treat on both counts. By the time the track was re-named as One Love and released again under the Prodigy's own name, the band's critics were obliged to accept that they were dealing with substantially more than a kiddie rave outfit whose time had past, and their supporters were every bit as surprised as Liam hoped. One Love pointed the way forward, towards ever harder beats, ever more complex structures, ever more eclectic influences and an ever more impressive wall of sound.

Aware that it had been several months since their last (official) release and that, in the wake of the fiasco in the States, they had taken a well-deserved sabattical from playing live, the band embarked on an extensive round of PAs to support the release of the single. Liam was delighted at the response to his new direction, and promised more with the release of their second, as yet untitled, album:

"It's the 180 bpm breakbeats I've moved away from. The new album is as hardcore as anything I've written, but hard in a different way, a German techno way. But I still use breakbeats because I've always been into hip hop, and that side of me will always be there."

While the new LP simmered away, however, the Prodigy had become embroiled in the politicisation of rave. As the scene had itself begun to diversify and expand, the hostility of the authorities grew with it; the band who still insisted that the buzz was really all they cared about were confronted with the fact that it could be taken away from them at any moment. Their first experience of government legislation designed to break up the party had come before the band were even formed, with the establishment of drugs squads specifically aimed at the free parties and raves, with many, such as the infamous party at Castle Morton, broken up by a police presence which would have been more appropriate during an armed riot.

While the Prodigy as a whole were conscious of these constant infringement on people's rights to have a good time over the next few years, they found themselves directly affected while playing '93's Resurrection party, outside Edinburgh. There were over 12,000 present and the whole affair was swinging merrily, at least until the intervention of the local authorities, who had despatched an official to monitor sound levels. Despite the party being held in a place about as close to the middle of nowhere as you could hope to find, the promoters were threatened with heavy fines, lost licences and confiscated equipment, unless the Prodigy's volume was cut dramatically.

They had little choice but to comply, leaving the band more likely to be drowned out by conversation than rock the crowd. Even their stubborn refusal to give anything less than their all for an audience buckled as they tried, tinnily, to rescue the gig; they stormed off-stage halfway through the set, the only person not frustrated and angry the council official. Shortly afterwards, they issued an apology to everyone at Resurrection, combined with a statement to the press denouncing what they would go on to call Their Law. When One Love came out, the statement was re-printed on its sleeve; it was unequivocal in its outrage:

> **"Forget the authorities, you can't stop us, we're gonna keep the dance scene strong even if the world isn't. This is your day and no-one can take it away from you. The dance scene is too strong to disappear."**

With the introduction of the draconian Criminal Justice Bill, the Prodigy continued to express their dismay with the malicious and misguided policies of a malicious and misguided government. They contributed a track to 1994's Taking Liberties, a compilation released to draw attention to the effects of the CJB, and Liam went on to explain that, as far as he was concerned:

"It's a fact of life that every time the Conservatives are doing badly in the polls, they bring in some outrageous piece of legislation to prove to the middle class voters in the Home Counties that they're 'tough' on law and order."

It would be a mistake, however, to see the band as politically motivated. Their stated ambition has always been to put across their music and to allow people the chance to share in it: the basic ethos of the rave. They didn't see themselves as political in the slightest, it was just that if government legislation trod on their toes, they'd strike back, Liam telling the NME that:

"We don't want to step up on stage and go 'fuck the police', like NWA or someone. We want people to forget that. OK, we drop Their Law because the Criminal Justice Bill is something we feel quite strongly about, but dance music is about the buzz, it's not about being depressed about politics. Really, I could not give a fuck. I really don't care. I could not care. As long as I'm happy, as long as I'm writing music that I want to write, all I care about is our people who buy the records, and the band, and the music. Our scene really."

When the time had been right, the Prodigy had taken the opportunity to issue an unequivocal 'fuck you' to those who tried to destroy that scene; the music was where Liam's heart was, and it was about to take another step forward.

full throttle

LIAM HAD BEEN BUSY ABSORBING SOME EXTREMELY DIVERSE SOUNDS AS THE ANTICIPATION OF THE SECOND LP INTENSIFIED: techno and house from all over Europe and the U.S., funk, the Beastie Boys and, increasingly, a smattering of Nirvana and such aged gods of rawk as Ted Nugent and Deep Purple. Managing to overcome his first serious bout of writer's block, the new record was almost completed by the time No Good (Start the Dance) was released; it was a potentially risky tune to use as a taster for the album, with its trad techno beats and female vocal sample - remember, this was the era of 2 Unlimited- but it paid off. Closer inspection revealed a far more intricate arrangement than its predecessors, while the tune as a whole carried a much deeper edge than the likes of Charly.

People were certainly interested to see what Liam had come up with on this second LP, itself a concept still pretty much unheard of within the mercurial dance scene; hardly anyone, however, would have predicted it would be quite as enthralling as Music for the Jilted Generation (the title was a late decision, winning out over a shortlist which had included Music for Joyriders). Jilted was, at once, a defiant return to the underground, never less than hardcore in the truest sense, while also managing to challenge and delight its listeners with its invention. The majority of critics could barely contain themselves, with the NME declaring that:

"Liam Howlett is a complete pop genius."

And, indeed, it was consummate pop music: music that successfully walked the line between, on the one hand, immediacy and popularity and, on the other, credibility and creative authority. The album illustrated the breadth of Liam's songwriting without losing the sense of coherency which was so important to the band: Jilted Generation, like Experience, had initially been conceived of, however loosely, as an instrumental concept album.

Break and Enter started proceedings, fierce and futuristic, with a sample of breaking glass used as additional percussion (the live version would feature Maxim smashing a stage bottle over Keith's head at the beginning of the track); Voodoo People consolidated Liam's technique of combining experimentation - building the tune up from a guitar sample, and basing it around samples of 'real' instruments - while keeping things to the point and always danceable; Speedway (Theme From Fastlane) was ample proof that there were few who could knock out anything as sonically venomous as the Prodigy. The entire LP was almost cinematic in the images it conjured up in the listener, particularly with the closing Narcotic Suite, three tracks written as a unit, wrapping up the album with perhaps the Prodigy's finest moment until that point. Inspired by Liam's ability to write to his own mental images, the LP climaxed in a welter of drugged up mood swings, spanning the funky, flute-laden and very nearly jazz 3 Kilos, the unsettling, tripped out Skylined and, finally, Claustrophobic Sting's nightmarish collage of free-floating sampled voices and abstract sound; as a conclusion to such an epic album, it ranks up there with the The Beatles' churning, fucked up masterpiece Tomorrow Never Knows.

Once more the public agreed, the album entering the charts at number one, and, in its first week of release, outselling the next two most popular LPs combined. Already critically acclaimed, Jilted Generation also won the Prodigy recognition from the mainstream music business, with a nomination for the televised Mercury Music Prize, for album of the year. Ultimately, they were perhaps a bit much for the thirtysomething jury to handle, the award going instead to M People (oh dear), but for Liam, the band's refusal to play ball in the name of their career had been vindicated:

> **"With the Mercury Award, the fact that we were there was good enough for me, because all those other bands that were there have gone through the normal route...We've managed to get there in a different way."**

Over the next few months the Prodigy returned to their favourite form of expression, playing live, touring the UK as well as visiting countries as far apart - geographically and culturally- as Iceland and Japan, while releasing, first, Voodoo People and then Poison to promote the album. Poison, in particular, cemented their reputation as virtually untouchable when it came to producing hard dance which could double as pop classic, and was also notable for being the first single by the band to feature a vocal by one of their own, as Maxim informed us that not only did he have the enigmatic poison, he had the remedy as well. Boasting a malevolently steady, 104 bpm beat, Liam's acknowledgement of his debt to hip hop, Poison demonstrated that it was possible to slow things right down while, if anything, making the overall effect even more menacing.

The song's video provided yet more evidence that the Prodigy were now a very different proposition to the green and white suited ravers who had brought the world Charly and Everybody In The Place. While the earlier videos were low budget affairs featuring Leeroy and Keith giving it some in a variety of locations, while Maxim looked on imperiously and Liam just looked mildly embarrassed, portraying the band as laugh-a-minute Essex nutters, the visuals that accompanied Poison had more in common with Clive Barker and cyberpunk.

The video for Poison saw director Walter Stern -responsible for each of the Prodigy's promos from No Good onwards - found the band in what can only be described as a dungeon, black sludge and cable wiring hanging from the walls, illuminated only by an irregular strobe. Maxim stands with his mic, rolling and shaking to the rhythm of the tune, hammered out by Liam, isolated behind a drum kit at the back of the set. Leeroy just stands, chewing gum, in shades despite the darkness. So far, so weird: enter Keith, his hair matted and his face encrusted with dirt. Between looming close ups of each band member, Maxim and Leeroy just seemingly just inches away from butting the camera, the light on, then off, Keith starts by squaring up to Leeroy, despite their marked difference in height, then chooses to taunt Liam, who observes him with distaste as he sets about the kit.

As the tune grows inexorably harsher and heavier, Liam leaps from his drums to attack his bandmate, pushing Keith into the squalor where he is left, crawling away from the rest of the Prodigy on all fours, a gimp, covered from head to toe in the noxious ooze that fills the room. Must have gone down a treat on the Saturday

morning Chart Show. Still, things were looking up for Keith: the video for Voodoo People had seen him as a ritual sacrifice, stuck inside a suitcase and left for dead.

The excellence of their videos was important for the Prodigy, not just because of their insistence on everything they're involved in coming up to scratch, but also because of their steadfast refusal to do TV. This wasn't limited to Top of the Pops; they would also turn down any other music programme that approached them, figuring that the confines of a TV studio would do little except dilute their frenzied live performance. The band, particularly Liam, don't make a secret of their control freak tendencies, and, although it may have pissed off the occasional TV producer, you couldn't say their hands-on perfectionism has let them down so far:

"We're not doing any telly. We just said bollocks, because we like to use everyone else's mistakes to improve our own thing. You know, just watching other bands on telly and seeing how shit they come across, because you can't project yourself the way you want to on TV...The videos are there to project the band, so are the live shows and the festivals. I reckon that's all people need really." - Liam

what evil lurks

THE THING ABOUT THE PRODIGY IS, they know how things work for them, and they know their own worth, and, as the Resurrection/Criminal Justice Bill episode showed, they aren't afraid of fighting their corner. Their attitude towards both TV and the press is a case in point; despite the majority of the music press hailing them as geniuses, especially after Jilted Generation, they have in the past received at least their share of critical abuse, with the virtual hate campaign run against them by Mixmag, in the band's early days, taking the biscuit.

They'd given Everybody In The Place a bad review, accusing it of being:

"A record made for children, by children...it's not underground unless you take my advice and bury it."

Bad reviews were an occupational hazard though, you couldn't sob quietly in a corner over one bad review of one single. What was to follow was something else entirely.

With Liam well out of the public eye, tucked away in the studio writing what would soon become Experience, he must have been surprised to find out he was on the cover of Mixmag. Surprise swiftly became fury, however, when he saw that the cover shot was a photo of him holding a gun to his head, a pose he'd done as a joke and one which the photographer had assured him would remain just that. Worse, the reason he was on the cover was to illustrate an article in that month's issue which, while purporting to examine the decline and fall of rave, in reality amounted to not much more than a lengthy, and rather bitter, attack on The Prodigy as both musicians and people.

55

Under the headline "Did Charly Kill Rave?", the piece
began by claiming that Liam was directly responsible
for the wave of cringeworthy rave-alongs which had
recently invaded the charts, all boasting gimmicky
references to children's TV: SesamE Street, A Trip to
Trumpton and, possibly worst of all, Roobarb and
Custard. In its desperation to have a go at the
Prodigy, Mixmag failed to point out that Charly had
come out over a year before these unfortunate novelty
hits, and that the band were already moving way
beyond it musically. As far as they were concerned:

"Rave is dead and they killed it."

Rather than mention the exploitative promoters and the greed which
really had begun to destroy rave, the article simply continued its
slagging of the Prodigy, with a series of personal jibes aimed at Keith
and the general implication that the band were nothing more than
chancers:

*"The ultimately cheesy teen rave act, the epitome of
rave, overground, Essex style, who make simple,
obvious and always over the top rave tunes."*

Apart from such displays of bad writing, the article also ended up
saying more about Mixmag than it did the Prodigy. After all, it was far
easier to criticise them than it was to admit that the reason they were

consistently popular wasn't because they were tacky, it was because they were good. In attacking Liam and the band, Mixmag may have been trying to exert some influence over the dance scene, but, fortunately, most people weren't that easily led. It was just a shame that some people in the scene obviously preferred it when nobody else liked dance music other than them and their mates. Liam later incinerated a copy of Mixmag during the video for, you guessed it, Fire, but, by then, it was already clear that the magazine had failed in its attempt to damage the Prodigy.

Five years later, and the vast majority of the press can say nothing but good things about the band. But, even now, the Prodigy are wary, sticking firmly by the old adage that, as they were quoted in Sky magazine:

"The press just build you up to tear you down."

They do however, at least for the moment, have the kind of support most bands would kill for, from the weekly music press, to metal mags such as Kerrang!, to Smash Hits and its ilk, all the way through to the music sections of serious-minded national newspapers. Even so, after the grief with Mixmag, who can blame them for still being just the slightest bit guarded? Despite rarely giving interviews, and refusing point blank to deal with what they see as the teen mags, the Prodigy post-Jilted Generation had to get used, however grudgingly, to the fact that they were now, in the eyes of the media, fully-fledged celebrities.

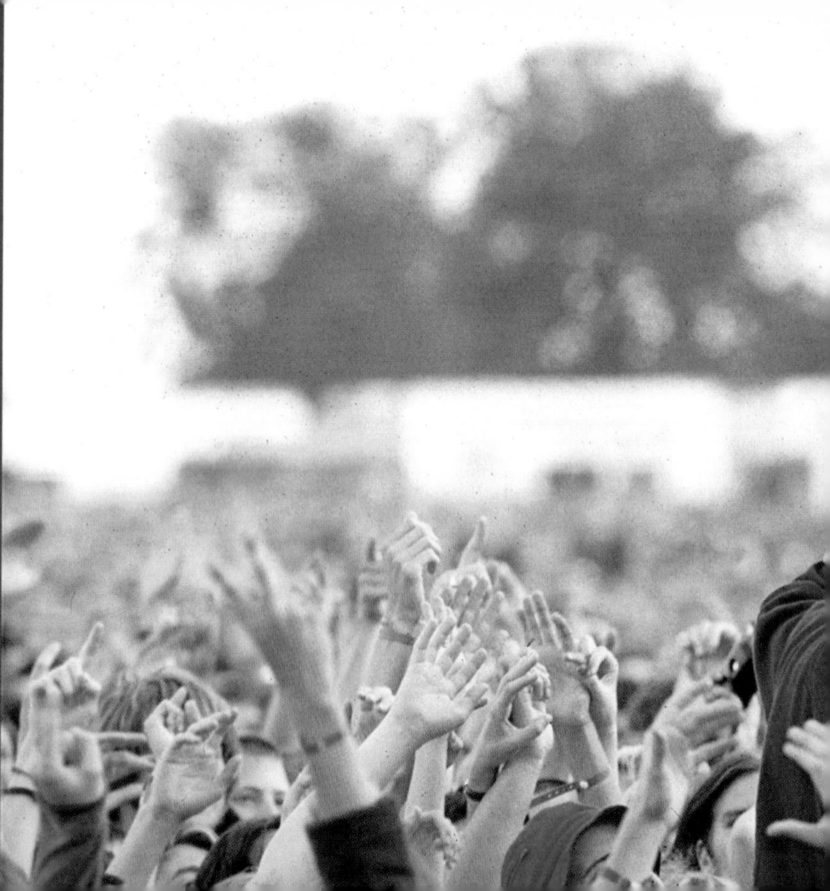

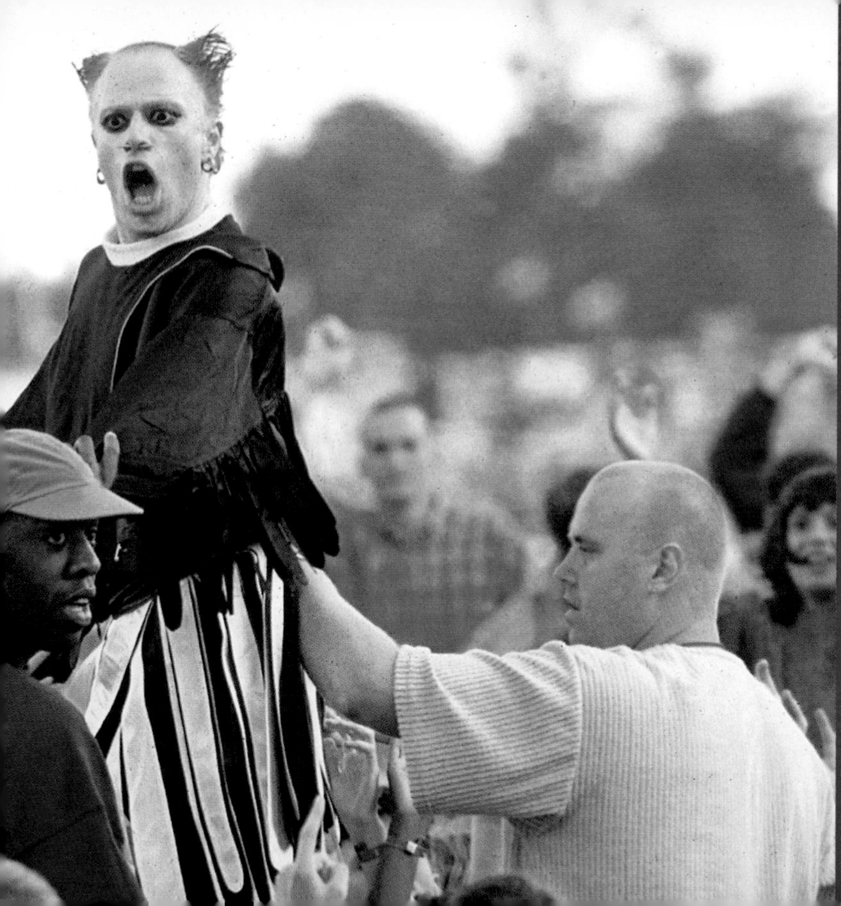

bad for you

bad for you
bad for you
bad for you

"I think I sometimes worry too much about trying to be credible and underground." - Liam

FOLLOWING THE RELEASE OF THE SECOND LP, the band took themselves back out on tour, while attempting to adjust to their new-found star status. Ambivalent at best about the fame which accompanied their growing popularity, the Prodigy did their best to avoid compromise, to prevent themselves coming off like just another parade of vacant, self-obsessed pop star celebs. Liam has described their apathy towards the media circuit as stemming from their own healthy sense of independence, saying that:

"People don't realise that we could have done a lot more than we've actually done in the way of making money, selling out in a way, doing shit local TV, loads and loads of interviews, but we don't because we want to try and control it."

As for the trappings of fame, the band walk the line between gratitude for the support of their real fans, while remaining resolutely unmoved by the attentions of those who dig them simply because everyone else does:

"It's a pain in the arse sometimes, but I'm not really bothered...Sometimes people like to show how into it they are, but if they get too excited I can't relate to it, and I'm probably not polite about it." - Keith

The summer of '95 saw the Prodigy taking a further step in their transition from a band involved in making superb dance music exclusively for the dance music scene, to one who made superb dance music for, well, just about everybody. The broadening of their musical horizons co-incided with a move away from club-based PAs and into the world of festivals, playing for crowds for whom they would probably represent a first taste of the dance underground.

Their storming of the summer festivals began with Glastonbury; they had originally wanted to play the previous year's festival, but had been overlooked in favour of Orbital. At the time Liam, who had, in the past, stuck rigorously to a policy of not dissing other bands in public, was notably unimpressed by this decision:

*"I don't like putting other bands down, but you'd
need to be on 30 mushrooms and at least a couple
of acid to have fun watching that."*

In the event, playing Glastonbury turned out to be nothing
short of a triumph. The show combined their expertise at
rocking an audience in the tens of thousands, accrued from
playing the likes of Raindance before they'd even released
What Evil Lurks, with the headfuck sound of their new set,
drawn largely from Jilted Generation. The Prodigy ignored
the staunchly indie atmosphere of the festival; to them,
the same principles applied whether they were playing
Glastonbury, Raindance or a tea dance at the local vicarage
- get the people moving, and keep them moving.

They followed Glastonbury with similarly swaggering
performances at Glasgow's T in the Park festival, the Melody
Maker subsequently dubbing them "one of the finest groups in
the country", before going on to play at that autumn's Tribal
Gathering. With this trio of festival appearances, the Prodigy proved
they were as good as their word, putting into practice their
commitment to play for any audience, to blow that audience away, and
share a bill with anyone who took their fancy. Liam had already widened his
favourite listening beyond the narrow confines of dance, and the band were by
now regularly playing alongside rock bands, indie bands, metal bands, and Bulgarian
folk bands (ok, the last one's a lie).

This willingness to try and
bring ever more divergent parts of the
musical spectrum into the Prodigy scheme of
things was again illustrated by their participation in
spring '96's Big Day Out, an Australian travelling festival in
the mould of Lollapalooza. For the next few weeks, they got
away from the British winter in style, sharing stage-space with the
likes of Porno for Pyros, Nick Cave and Rage Against The Machine.

With Gizz the guitarist in tow, increasingly covered in tattoos and
piercings, the band were, both musically and visually, a long way indeed
from the fresh faced ravers from Braintree who'd busted out with Charly
and Everybody in the Place. The rock audiences were offered the
challenge of converting an entirely new crowd, rather than simply playing
for an audience who were already smitten with them, while playing
before established heavy rock bands spurred them on to ever-more
bonecrushimgly intense musical heights. Keith expressed this
sentiment after a series of such shows around Europe:

*"We started off playing at the clubs we used to go to, but because we've all been
in loads of different scenes - I've been playing in rock scenes, know what I
mean? - what was much better was playing the places we shouldn't be playing at.
And that's what we did. We thought 'fuck it', got on the bill with Senser,
Biohazard, Helmet, Suicidal Tendencies and the Red Hot Chilli Peppers. Barbed
wire round the stage, no glo-sticks, no Vicks, people spitting everywhere,
brilliant. We went there, rocked it, and held our heads up."*

the progression of their sound and that of their shows went hand in hand. While still a hip hop boy at heart, he had already shown with the move from Cut to Kill to the Prodigy that his talents weren't restricted to making formularised, genre sounds:

"I guess you're just influenced by who you see...We just got bored with the typical sound of the dance scene, and wanted to expand on that, and that just happened to be the way we went. It wasn't like a decision to get heavier."

From their roots in rave and techno, the Prodigy were rapidly becoming a genuine rock n'roll band. And a pretty damn good one at that.

"Rock music is an attitude - it's not about 'You've got to have guitars'." - Liam

fire starting

fire fire starting
fire starting starting

"There's nothing pop about the Prodigy whatsoever. We might be popular...but that's a total accident - we didn't go out there looking for it." - Keith

IN THE WORDS OF A BRITISH MUSIC BIZ EXECUTIVE, the Prodigy's next release was the one which "sent them nuclear". Even more than during the hiatus after Experience, Jilted Generation had succeeded in whetting people's appetites, eager to see what Liam could come up with next; once again, he surpassed expectations.

From its first bar onwards, Firestarter proved to be yet another massive stylisic leap onwards for the Prodigy, and not simply for the quality of its beats, providing the foundation for a dense and claustrophobic three-and-a-half minute instant classic single. The first time many people heard the tune, including a sampled snatch of guitar by The Breeders and a few scattered 'hey's from the Art of Noise's Close to the Edit, was after it had already entered the charts at number one, uncharted territory for the band.

Even when compared to Jilted, Firestarter managed to be both compelling and immediate while, if anything, creating an even darker sound than its predecessors; for the nation's favourite single, it was an epically aggressive tune, bordering on the psychotic. So, this was what Liam had been tinkering around with in the studio.

As, musically, Firestarter revolved around an oppressive sense of disorientation and dementia, who better to give it human form than Keith? While Maxim had played frontman on Poison, now it was Keith's turn and, boy, did he make the most of it. He was the Firestarter - the twisted Firestarter - spitting and snarling his incendiary message. The video was another almost cinematic, definitely nightmarish venture into the band's psyche, finding Keith alone in a barren, monochrome service tunnel, staring out the camera, and by implication anyone watching the video. Physically, Keith personified the moodswing which had come over the Prodigy, one which articulated itself with Firestarter.

In the band's videos, he had already completed the transition from cuddly, long-haired raver to the gimp of Poison, but this time he made an even more arresting sight; his hair was now cut into twin mohicans on either side of his head, he looked at the world through a haze of eyeliner, his nose and tongue pierced and bolted. The clown of the Prodigy had now evidently got sick in the head.

If the video for Firestarter made a hero out of Keith, the single itself gave the band yet more critical and commercial plaudits, as Liam was hailed as the voice of the disillusioned and disenchanted, obviously a serious musical talent on a journey somewhere very, very dark and nasty, but all without losing the popularity which took Firestarter to number one not only in Britain, but six other European countries too. On top of all that, the single, with Keith's vocal at its centre, signified in large measure just why their appeal kept on growing: chemistry. The band not only made great records, each member had now reached the stage where their individual personalities were apparent: Liam, the quiet, almost reclusive man behind the music, the genius foundation of the Prodigy; Maxim, the godfather, cutting an impressively daunting figure on record, stage and video; Leeroy, still bouncing to the beat, however dark it got; and Keith. Keith had always been Keith, but now he was the madman focal point of the whole thing, tunes, live, the works, rather than just another visual to adorn the stage show.

This development of character was ample proof that the Prodigy had mastered another of the tricks of becoming a genuinely great rock band, amplifying themselves through the music to create an image which, while striking, was still, ultimately, just the way they were. All the great bands had this element of personality, and now the Prodigy did too, but without the pomposity and bullshit that often comes along for the ride. As Liam had said earlier, the Prodigy learnt from other's mistakes, and they were Grade A students:

"People love Keith for being mad. He's the celebrity of the band, just because of the way he is. And people love Leeroy for...whatever he does. Maxim's a bit more than that. Maxim, OK, he dances, but he's had his moment of glory with Poison. And they'll both have their moments of glory on the new album."

Like a number of great bands before them, however, the Prodigy discovered that one of the downsides of the kind of success they were having came in the form of yet more aggro with the media. But, on this occasion, the problem wasn't a slating in Mixmag, the grief came from certain sections of the national press, who purposefully grasped the wrong end of the stick, accusing Firestarter of being an anthem for arsonists. The Mail On Sunday was among the first to try and whip up a spot of hysteria among the grannies, running a piece on the band and the single which was headlined:

"BAN THIS SICK FIRE RECORD!"

Although Firestarter remained firmly unbanned, the article succeeded in bringing the band the unwanted attentions of the usual suspects within Britain's attempt at a moral majority; the BBC received a number of complaints about showing the video on Top of the Pops, partially as a result of the Mail On Sunday's 'exposure' of the band as advocates of arson, and, in addition, supposed unease about the disturbing effect of the video on the nation's youth when shown at 7 O'clock on a Thursday evening or, for that matter, played at ear-splitting volume by Joe the schizophrenic during an episode of Eastenders. The furore over Firestarter climaxed with a question being asked in the House of Commons, anxiously appealing for a debate over this no-doubt pernicious and insurrectionary racket sitting atop the charts. The band, for their part, seemed vaguely amused by the whole episode, with Keith saying at the time:

"It's a joke though, innit? I mean, if you write a song which said something as blatant as that, and it did happen, then you'd write songs that went 'Give me money, give me fucking money, give me really nice clothes, give me really cool drugs, give me money."

Sounds like a winner to me...

fuel the fire

BACK IN THE REAL WORLD, The Prodigy went on to build on their successes at the previous year's summer festivals, repeating - and bettering - the trick by headlining Phoenix, Reading, T in the Park, the Brighton Music Festival and the Feile, as well as providing main support for Oasis at their shows at Knebworth; Liam was certainly fulfilling his stated ambition to get his tunes across, as their presence at these festivals put them in front of, collectively, hundreds of thousands of people.

They later went out on another tour of the UK (complete with their 'Living Room' set), before heading off round Europe, their schedule including a date at a Prague snowboard festival. Although, by this time, the band would have faced few problems in selling out such venues, they consistently refused to play conventional stadiums or arenas, both in Britain and abroad, still mindful of the debacle at Resurrection, and unwilling to have their carefully-constructed show diluted by clipboard-wielding officials wanting to impose restrictions on their sound levels.

By now, the Prodigy's policy of playing for rock audiences who may otherwise have short-sightedly written them off as catering solely for the dance scene was also beginning to pay off. Throughout the second half of '96, their gigs were packed not only with dance fans, but also people whose tastes ran the musical gamut. Like the best of the early raves, a Prodigy show was an inclusive event; their entire approach was based around not caring which particular sub-culture you came out of or what you listened to other than them - as long as the Prodigy rocked you, that was enough.

As if to emphasise the point, the band had started to close their performances with a raucous, techno and guitar cover version of L7's Fuel My Fire, with Liam commenting that:

"Ending on that note is just like 'fucking have this'."

since the Acid House era, numerous guitar bands had to incorporate technology and the dance sound into their music; the vast majority simply ended up as ham-fisted and embarrassing, achieving little besides sticking a few odd noises and samples over an otherwise bog standard rock song. The only band who had really made this tricky balancing act work had been one which had emerged from the dance scene, in the shape of the Prodigy, who managed to combine rock's rawness and urgency with the vitality and texture of dance music: and they made it all look so easy. As their festival appearances confirmed, audiences were quick to give them their due respect:

"We started as a rave act and tried to turn it around. There aren't many other acts that have really pulled that off. Punks, hippies, rockers, bikers, mods - you name 'em, they were down the front going mental."-
Liam

electronic punks

WHAT FIRESTARTER INITIATED, Breathe continued. Another fine tune, another entry to the chart at number one. Keith once more took the lead vocal, over the track's pounding compound of heavy guitars, even heavier beats and Liam's patented barrages of chilling, rollercoaster electronica. The synthesis of rock and dance was further perfected on Breathe; its rhythm track was comparable to the best hard house and techno, while Keith's sneering vocal reminded you of nothing so much as a prime time Johnny Rotten on God Save The Queen. Just like Firestarter, it made everyone with a love of modern music feel like an excitable adolescent again: to even the most jaded and cynical listener, the fact that something as awesomely nasty as this could get to number one was a matter for celebration, proving we hadn't all yet submitted to nostalgia and blandness.

Maybe that's the whole point of the Prodigy.

Walter Stern's video for Breathe again managed to capture just the right mood of paranoia and vexation, Keith and Maxim on either side of a single room's dividing wall, Keith attempting to batter it down to get at Maxim, who, whenever the camera was trained on him, simply glared at it through his cat's eye contacts, grinning the grin of a man with something extremely unpleasant to hide. The entire band were then shown in the same decrepit, filthy room, while a variety of household objects defied gravity, resting on the ceiling, between close-up shots of a centipede crawling slowly along a shelf of antiquated books, and a let's not forget the crocodile lurking in the room's darker recesses (just your average day round Liam's?). It was an array of thoroughly spooked imagery, cryptic, intimidating and hard to shake from your thoughts, an ideal accompaniment for a song which exhibited much the same qualities

The critical reaction to Breathe was suitably favourable. The praise of the music press was by now almost predictable, but the Prodigy had also began to take up column inches in the national press, and not only for articles such as the Mail on Sunday's. The Prodigy were now regarded as something of a phenomenon within the British music scene, a refreshing and innovative alternative to the glut of trad 'Dadrock' bands who were filling the airwaves. Liam, in particular, was beginning to merit attention as a serious talent, someone whose music was not only perfect for the present, but was pointing the way towards the future as well. In a review of Breathe, the Guardian went as far as to say that:

"Liam Howlett, one of the great musical wunderkids of the age, simply cannot stop himself writing astonishing songs."

The single, complete with Keith's mocking, drawled vocal delivery, was further evidence that the band were indeed the 'electronic punks' they claimed to be. Both their music and their attitude summed up the original nihilistic sentiments of punk, something which Liam acknowledged by saying:

"Punk rock is an attitude. Our attitude is 'here we are, you can fucking take it or leave it'. If that's punk rock, then we're punk rock."

wind it up

ALL THINGS CONSIDERED, '96 HAD BEEN A VINTAGE YEAR FOR THE PRODIGY, PROBABLY THEIR BEST YET. The only real blemish had, once again, involved the music press, although, on this occasion, it was the Prodigy - or at least Keith - who ended up in trouble. The grief had started with a March interview in the NME, during which Keith explained his indifference towards celebrity and the band's reluctance to appear on television:

"TV corrupts people. A lot of acts get that little break, and they change from T-shirt and shorts to designer stuff, swanning around like arseholes. I mean, to me, Goldie and Bjork are like that. Goldie's coming on like the bad boy of the jungle scene - from the underground and all that - and then the next thing you know, he's going on to give an award to his girlfriend at the Brit Awards. Now that to me was as sickening as Michael Jackson and Lisa Marie Presley. I'm not dissing him, right, but if I watch that, it's Bon Jovi. It's Hollywood. You give 'em a few front covers and they want to play the pop star game."

Goldie, perhaps predictably, took this rather badly, and so began a running feud, with animosity and tension between the two acts high throughout the rest of the year. Goldie was known to be furious at Keith's remarks, although he only made one public show of retaliation: sharing a bill with the Prodigy at the Brighton Music Festival, he came onstage sporting a T-shirt which featured a large reproduction of Keith's head, beneath the single word 'Cuntface'. Obviously not a happy man.

Despite Keith issuing a statement through XL arguing that he had been taken in by the NME journalist in question, who took his opinions on Goldie out of context, there seemed no way to heal the rift. Finally, for the Christmas edition of Musik, a meeting was arranged between Keith and Goldie, with a representative from the magazine acting as referee. Unfortunately for Keith, he got stuck in traffic, arriving for the showdown over an hour late, and, in the meantime, Goldie took the opportunity to give his side of the story:

"I was livid. I was going to send the boys round to his house. I eventually spoke to him and said 'Who the fuck are you...fuck off!'...It was so annoying. Grooverider wanted to punch his teeth out, Fabio wanted to kneecap him. It's total disrespect on his part, man...If people want to start having a go at us about it, we can go dancing, you know what I mean?"

It was an understandably edgy Keith who finally arrived at the South Kensington hotel where the meeting was being held. After a period of tension, the pair began to discuss matters; Keith apologised, explaining that he had been let down by the NME journalist, who had printed a misrepresented version of a conversation which was supposed to have been off-the-record anyway, adding that:

"You learn, though, don't you?"

After a while, things appeared to calm down, the two agreeing that the entire episode had been a case of extremely crossed wires, and was best left in the past; in fact, only one question continued bugging Goldie:

"What the fuck am I going to do with that fucking T-shirt now?"

The story got its happy ending: later that night, The Prodigy were presented with their MTV Europe Award for Best Dance Act by none other than Goldie, while Mixmag's front cover showed him and Keith, together, busily patching things up. XL subsequently released a statement to the effect that Keith and Goldie were now :

"Officially 'not pissed off' with each other".

The end of the feud came as a great relief for Keith:

"The worst thing about it all is that I consequently dragged the name of the Prodigy down through this shit. That really cut me up, because I'd do anything to protect the band...That Goldie, man, he's not the sort of bloke to get on the wrong side of... I thought it would come to blows at one stage...It's a closed chapter now, thank God."

The Prodigy as a whole were similarly glad to see the back of the ill feeling, although it's unlikely that the rumpus did much to improve their opinions on the music press.

wind it up

86

voodoo people

"It's just Prodigy music" - Liam

**THEIR MTV AWARD WASN'T THE ONLY ONE TO END UP
DECORATING THE BAND'S RESPECTIVE MANTELPIECES:** the
Prodigy also ended up bagging awards for Best Video and Best
Dance Act at the NME Brat Awards, while they recieved more
recognition from the music industry with Brits nominations for Best
Single and Best Video. Select also voted them Best Live Band, and
Keith may have been pleasantly surprised to learn that the same poll
had judged him not only among the Best Dressed of '96, but also the
fourth most popular "Person You'd Most Like To Do The Wild Thing With",
only pipped at the post by the likes of the Spice Girls and Liam Gallagher.
This was as good an indication as any that Keith had become really rather
famous, with there also being sightings, at gigs and on the streets, of growing
numbers of 'Keith clones'.

They again had to come to terms with the fact that getting two successive number ones had only
intensified the interest in them from the more scurrilous tabloids. According to the Daily Star, Liam and
Keith were close to finalising a deal to buy a Brighton radio station, while the same newspaper reported
that Keith had become engaged to model Catalina, star of TFI Friday. The story, funnily enough,
transpired as having little grounding in fact, although subsequent unsubstantiated rumours in the press
then decided that Catalina wasn't involved with Keith at all, but was in fact going out with Liam!

89

All this was probably of only mild interest to the band themselves, who had chosen to spend a second winter in Australia, where they returned to the stage of the Big Day Out. They otherwise kept themselves occupied hanging out and racing bikes with Barry Sheen; Keith, in particular, has long been a bike enthusiast, the proud owner of a CBK 900 Fireblade, reputed to be the fastest bike in the world. Liam, on the other hand, enjoys a spot of snowboarding, choosing Colorado as his favoured location, although he has advised that:

"If you're starting out, I'd recommend France or Switzerland, 'cause they're so into having a laugh."

Snowboarding and bikes aren't simply the pastimes of bored pop stars with too much time on their hands; their choice of leisure activities reflects their past, with Liam and Leeroy both having grown up with skateboards and BMXs, a culture tied up with the emergence of electro, breakdancing and the first wave of hip hop which Liam was so enamoured of. The one thing they probably weren't doing was going out clubbing, with Keith telling Hot Press that:

"I've stopped going to clubs, because 99% of what they play is bollocks."

Unfortunately, Britain was faced with the worrying possibility that the Prodigy may not resurface playing live until much later in the year, due to their increasingly full diary in America, where - largely thanks to them -British dance music seems to have finally caught on, MTV devoting a show to it following Firestarter's achievement of selling well over 100,000 copies on import alone. Their fondness for Glastonbury may win out in the end, however.

At least by then, we'll have discovered just what Liam's had in store for us. After much to-ing and fro-ing, by the time you read this, The Fat Of The Land will be out, recorded at Liam's own Braintree studio, Earthbound. The third album has been the subject of intense debate, with interested parties wondering just what it's going to sound like, just who will be appearing on it besides the regular band members and, until recently, just what it'll be called (speculation among fans on the internet had previously guessed at Blow Your Mind or Year 2000 as possible candidates). Like Experience and Jilted Generation, the LP has been written around Liam's ideal that an album should be able to encompass a variety of styles and influences, without losing its own internal logic:

"I think singles have to be pretty up...an album's different, because you don't have to pack everything into a four-minute tune - you've got the space to experiment and demonstrate your full range of ideas."

Liam's eventual choice of collaborators has offered yet more proof of the fiercely eclectic nature of his and the Prodigy's tastes, as well as their acknowledgement of, and respect for, their own musical heritage. Apart from the album's instrumentals, and those tracks featuring vocals by Keith and Maxim, the guest appearance of Kula Shaker's Crispian Glover testifies that the band are now very much at ease working with rock music and rock musicians, Liam's love of guitars bringing forth more inspiration. Elsewhere, the band make a nod back to the influence of hip hop, with one tune built around a rap by Dr. Octagon a.k.a Kool Keith, previously a member of the Ultramagnetic MC's, still a favourite of Liam's, who he publicly expressed his admiration for in the pages of the Melody Maker as long ago as 1993.

Just in case anyone wonders where all this leaves the former kings of rave, the recorded version of Fuel My Fire comes with vocals by Republica's Saffron; while, at the time of writing, it was unclear whether the cut would be included on the finished article, it's interesting to note that Saffron's career began with one of the Prodigy's earliest contemporaries, N Joi. And, let's face it, you only need to listen to Breathe or Firestarter to realise that it's not as if Liam's forgotten how to write some of the hardest, most well crafted dance tunes you could wish to treat your ears to.

93

That's the deal with the Prodigy: they've got a sense of history, without being in any way restricted by it. At times, it's as if forty years of rock n'roll has been compressed into one voice, one band, and yet all without ever sounding derivative, or indeed, less than relentlessly inventive. Elvis, The Beatles, early Mantronix, Parliament, The Stooges, the Sex Pistols, Phuture, Derrick May and Slayer; it's possible to hear all of them in the Prodigy, but it's not necessarily even directly audible. It seeps through the grooves of the vinyl in terms of attitude, the fuck you sensibility which informs the tunes and defies categorisation.

The Prodigy have proved themselves. time and again, to be virtually the only people capable of expressing the real range of what is, ultimately not punk, or techno, or metal, or hip hop, but rock and roll. Moreover, they've done all this without losing sight of the importance of the show, the importance of giving a crowd something to be dazzled by and something to remember. Again, it's a line which stretches back from Presley right through to Raindance, Perception and the outdoor all-nighters which brought them together. The band, though they'd be reluctant to admit it, are stars, not because they've set out to be, boring us rigid with tedious tales of drugs and celebrity marriages; they've become icons for our Jilted Generation simply through being themselves.

And yet they never sound anything other than new - what Liam and the band dream up in the studio becomes, more often than not, a sure sign of the way forward, whether within dance (listen to the proto-jungle breakbeats on Experience, and reflect on just what drum and bass came out of), or within music as a whole (the diverse influences which mean, as Liam has pointed out, that the Prodigy's music can only really be called just that - Prodigy music). Great leaps forward usually come from Liam's tried and tested method of imbibing as many different sounds as possible; although it frequently horrifies purists from every genre, the best music is usually mongrel by birth. But, for Liam, it's no big deal; it's just the way he does things:

"To use a cliché - we've got a rock and roll attitude. I love jungle and hip hop because they're human, and I also love loud, wailing guitars",

while, for Keith, his bandmate's songwriting talents mean total freedom for the band as a whole:

"Now we don't have to blend in with anything. We can be as heavy as we like."

Great music usually comes from the most unlikely places. It's not always the supposedly artistic, cosmopolitan major cities that produce the real visionaries; it's worthwhile keeping an eye on the small towns and the suburbs as well. Likewise, the best bands frequently emerge from scenes which at the time are dismissed as passing fads with no future.

You've only got to look at the Prodigy: who would have thought that the quietly-spoken B-Boy turned raver with the C90 full of his home-made tunes would turn out to be probably the greatest songwriter of his time. Or that, while the music industry hung around at the bar at a million desperate London pub gigs, that the future was, in fact, being brought to life at an outdoor party in nearby Essex? Well, that's the way it happened, and that's the way it looks like staying. The Prodigy: the last great rock and roll band on the planet.

96